# Great Journeys Across Earth

# MARCO POLO'S TRAVELS ON ASIA'S SILK ROAD

## Cath Senker

Heinemann Library

Chicago, Illinois

© 2008 Heinemann Library
a division of Reed Elsevier Inc.
Chicago, Illinois

Customer Service  888-454-2279
Visit our website at www.heinemannraintree.com

Produced for Heinemann Library by
Monkey Puzzle Media Ltd.

Designed by Jane Hawkins and Victoria Bevan.

Originated by Modern Age.
Printed and bound in China

12 11 10 09 08
10 9 8 7 6 5 4 3 2 1

**Library of Congress Cataloging-in-Publication
Data**
Senker, Cath.
   Marco Polo's travels on Asia's Silk Road / Cath
Senker.
      p. cm. -- (Great journeys across Earth)
   Includes bibliographical references and index.
   ISBN-13: 978-1-4034-9751-2 (hb) --
   ISBN-13: 978-1-4034-9759-8 (pb)
1.  Polo, Marco, 1254-1324--Juvenile literature. 2.
Asia--Description and travel--Juvenile literature.
3.  Explorers--Portugal--Biography--Juvenile
literature. I. Title.
G370.P9S46 2007
915.04'2092--dc22
[B]
                                    2007005835

**Acknowledgments**
The author and publisher are grateful to the
following for permission to reproduce copyright
material: akg-images pp. **5, 9, 20–21** (Ullstein/
Kanus), **27**; Art Archive pp. **26, 28** (Musée
Cernuschi Paris/Dagli Orti), **33** (Bodleian Library
Oxford), **39**; Bridgeman Art Library p. **19** (Topkapi
Palace Museum, Istanbul, Turkey/Giraudon); Corbis
pp. **4** (Keren Su), **7** (Archivo Iconografico S.A.), **12**
(Burstein Collection), **15** (Michael S. Yamashita), **23**
(Pierre Colombel), **41** (Bettmann); Getty Images pp.
**10** (Robert Harding World Imagery), **11, 29** (AFP),
**31** (Photographer's Choice), **34** (Bridgeman Art
Library), **37** (Hulton Archive); Mary Evans Picture
Library p. **14**; North Wind Picture Archives pp. **1, 25,
38**; Still Pictures p. **13** (Oldrich Karasek); Topfoto
pp. **8** (HIP), **16–17** (Alinari), **18, 22** (ImageWorks), **36**
(Roger-Viollet).

Maps by Martin Darlison at Encompass Graphics.

Cover photograph of desert sand dunes
reproduced with permission of Alamy
(Jef Maion/Nomads' Land).

Title page picture: Marco, Niccolo, and Matteo
Polo are welcomed at the court of the Mongol
ruler Kublai Khan in May 1275.

Expert read by Dr. Paulette Posen, environmental
research scientist at the University of East Anglia,
United Kingdom.

# Contents

Desert Hardships   4

The Polos' Two Journeys   6

Into the Mongol Realm   10

Toward the Silk Road   18

The Land of the Great Khan   24

In the Service of the Khan   30

The Journey Home   34

Marco's Book   38

The Polos' Adventures in Asia   42

Timeline   44

Glossary   46

Further Information   47

Index   48

Some words are shown in bold, **like this**. You can find out what they mean by looking in the glossary.

# Desert Hardships

More than 700 years ago, in 1272, Marco Polo traveled slowly through the desert in Iran. He was with his father, Niccolo, and uncle, Matteo (Maffeo), but there were no signs of other people, water, or food. The three relied on supplies carried by their camels. They suffered from scorching heat by day and freezing temperatures at night.

The Polos kept a constant watch for gangs of robbers, which were common in those areas. They cautiously entered the land of the Karaunas, a violent robber tribe. For protection, they joined a large **caravan** (group of travelers).

### Deserts hot and cold

*During the day in a desert, the Sun's rays heat up the land. At night there are no clouds to act as a blanket and keep in the heat. The heat rises high into the sky, and the land temperature falls to below the freezing point. In some Iranian deserts, the daytime temperature can reach 104°F (40°C), while at night it is 19°F (-7°C).*

These people are traveling in a modern-day camel caravan. But the scene is very similar to Marco Polo's travels across Asia many centuries ago.

## Battle in the sand

Suddenly, a dust storm struck. Sand and dust whirled around, and the caravan had to halt. Now the cunning Karaunas took their opportunity to attack. The travelers unsuccessfully tried to fight back. In the struggle, dust, and confusion, the Polos managed to escape. But other travelers were seized as **slaves** and would never see their loved ones again.

### The slave trade

*During the Middle Ages in Europe, Africa, and Central Asia, people captured in battle were sold in slave markets to the rich and powerful. Slaves worked for their masters for no money. Marco Polo himself had a Mongol slave named Peter, who was freed after Marco died.*

This painting from 200 years ago shows slave owners buying and selling slaves at the market in Egypt. The scene would have been very similar in Marco's time.

This was just one adventure from the Polos' long, long journey. They traveled from their home in Venice, Italy, all the way across Asia to China and back again. Marco wrote an exciting book about the trip, which most people at the time did not believe. How did they manage to survive such an amazing adventure—and how much of Marco's book was true?

# The Polos' Two Journeys

The Polo family came from the wealthy port of Venice, Italy. Marco's father and uncle were adventurous **merchants**, prepared to travel the world to make money. In 1253 they sailed to Constantinople (now Istanbul, Turkey) on business. From there, in about 1259, the fearless pair set off east to the Mongol lands, which were unknown to Europeans.

Niccolo and Matteo Polo took a northerly route to China on their first trip from 1253 to 1269. The Mongol Empire covered much of Asia. The four regions of the empire are shaded on the map.

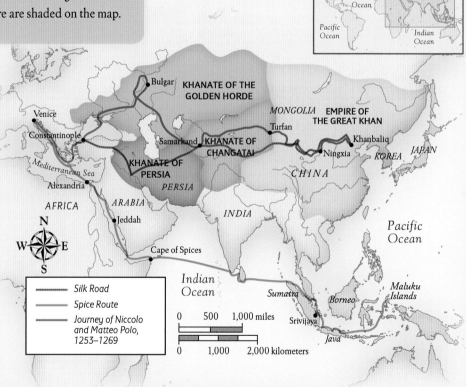

## Silk Road and Spice Route

Precious goods from Asia, such as **silks**, spices, and gemstones, were brought huge distances to Europe along two main routes. The Silk Road was not a single, well-marked road, but rather several overland tracks from China to Europe, stretching an incredible distance of over 4,000 miles (6,500 kilometers). Even longer was the Spice Route, a sea journey from East and Southeast Asia, past India to the Middle East and Europe.

After six years of travel across Asia, the Polo brothers met the ruler, or **khan**, of the entire **Mongol Empire**. He was named Kublai Khan, or the Grand Khan. He had never seen Europeans before and was curious to know about them. He welcomed the Polos to stay in his magnificent palace in Khanbaliq (now Beijing, in China).

## The Polos return

In about 1266, homesick after so many years away, Niccolo and Matteo set off back to Venice. They had promised to carry out an important mission back in Europe for Kublai Khan. Then, they would return to see him again in China.

### Under Mongol rule

*The Mongols came from the northeast **steppes** (grasslands) of Asia. Before the Polos' time, the Mongol leader Genghis Khan, grandfather of Kublai Khan, had conquered a huge area, which had been divided into four regions. Genghis Khan gave his enemies two choices: lay down your arms and accept our rule or die. Those who accepted Mongol rule were allowed to continue their customs.*

Venice, in the south of Europe on the Adriatic Sea (part of the Mediterranean), was a perfect place for trading. Merchants exchanged goods with other European lands and with Russia to the northeast, across the Mediterranean Sea with North Africa, and eastward with the Middle East and Asia.

## The Polos set out

Niccolo and Matteo returned to Venice in 1269. Niccolo discovered that his wife had died just after he had left, while giving birth to their son, Marco. Now 15 years old, Marco was overjoyed to see his long-lost father. On the next trip, he would accompany Niccolo and Matteo.

## Marco Polo's early life

After Marco's mother died, he had probably been brought up, as a baby and then a child, by his aunt and uncle. As the son of a successful and wealthy merchant, he had a good education. He studied the writers of ancient Greece and Rome. He read the Bible and learned French. In his free time, he played outdoors with his cousins and rowed on the Venice canals.

## A mission for the Grand Khan

In the summer of 1271, the Polos set sail for Acre, in modern-day Israel. They loaded their ship with bedding, clothes, water, wine, and food that would survive a long voyage— salted meat, cheese, and dry crackers. They were armed in case of pirate attack.

The Polos arrived safely in Acre and traveled to Jerusalem to obtain **holy oil** from an important church. The oil was for Kublai Khan, who liked to collect special things from different religions in faraway places.

In Acre the Polos also delivered a letter from Kublai Khan to the pope, the head of the Christian Catholic Church.

The Polo brothers Niccolo and Matteo, with Niccolo's son Marco, set sail from Venice in 1271.

Kublai Khan's letter asked for 100 educated European men to travel back to China with the Polos. Then, Kublai Khan could learn about Christianity and the ways and customs of European people. But the pope allowed just two unwilling **priests** to leave with the Polos on their expedition.

## Acre

*Acre was an important port with a sheltered **harbor** for ships. But today, the harbor is clogged with mud and silt. These tiny particles are easily carried by moving water, but settle on the bottom in still water. Acre's harbor can now be used only by small fishing boats.*

Pope Gregory X asked the Polos to meet him in Acre. He said he would help them.

## The threat of war

Soon after the travelers left Acre, they heard that war had broken out in Armenia, which was the region they were about to cross. Terrified, the priests turned back. But the Polos carried on, and in late 1271 they made their way through the dangerous country.

# Into the Mongol Realm

The Polos continued their journey east through Kurdistan, near the towering Mount Ararat. By now it was 1272. They traveled on southward to Mosul and Baghdad in Iraq. Baghdad was an important center for trade, science, and law. From Iraq the adventurers moved on to Saba in present-day Iran. They were now in the **Mongol Empire**.

Mount Ararat is an extinct or "dead" volcano in eastern Turkey. Its peak is 16,853 feet (5,137 meters) high and covered in snow all year. Kurdish people move their cattle and sheep between the valleys in winter and the upper slopes in the summer.

## Religions of the Mongol Empire

During the Polos' time, each region of the Mongol Empire had its own ruler, or **khan**, who was loyal to Kublai Khan. As long as people obeyed his rule, Kublai Khan allowed them to follow their own religion. There were Christians, Jews, Muslims, **Buddhists**, and followers of many other religions.

## The nomad tradition

The Mongols came from the grasslands, or **steppes**. These areas were not suited to farming or building villages, but they were good for grazing animals. The Mongols were **nomads**—people who moved from place to place. They traveled with their horses, cattle, and other animals, continually looking for fresh grass and water supplies. To this day, nomads live on the Mongolian steppes.

As the Mongols moved beyond their homelands, they traded with villagers and townspeople for food, tools, and other goods that nomads cannot easily produce. They also traded with foreigners in their empire. They always made sure that people obeyed the Mongol rule of law.

### Black oil

*Marco heard about a strange thick liquid called black oil. It came from pools and wells around Baku, on the shore of the Caspian Sea, to the north of their route. Local people burned the oil in lamps and smeared it on the skin to treat diseases. Baku is still an important petroleum, or oil-producing, area today.*

Marco heard about oil found in Baku. Today, a large amount of oil is produced there and sold to other countries. The oil is under the ground, reached by drilling deep wells using towers called derricks.

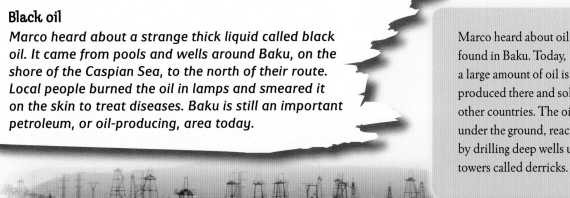

## Creating an empire

The Mongols had conquered a huge empire because their armies moved quickly and their soldiers fought fiercely. The Mongols loved horses and were amazingly skilled riders. Marco heard that Mongol riders could stay in the saddle for 48 hours at a time, even sleeping there while their horses grazed! The warriors traveled light and could live for a month on mares' (female horses') milk and wild animal flesh. In battle, Mongol **archers** on horseback galloped toward the enemy while firing arrows.

### Fighting backwards

Marco described how the Mongols sometimes fought while they seemed to be retreating:

"They pretend to flee, shooting arrows backwards, so killing as many men and horses as if they were fighting face to face!"

Mongols practiced their fierce fighting on horseback, using bows and arrows or swords and spears.

## Severe punishment

The Mongols lived by strict rules. Punishments for crimes were severe. Robbers were beaten with a cane up to 100 times, and many died of their wounds. Stealing a horse was extremely serious, and the culprit was cut in two by a sword. However, wealthy criminals could avoid punishment by paying back nine times the value of the stolen goods.

## Daily life

When they were not at war, Mongol men lived with their families in *yurts*, which are round tents made from wool and horsehair. One man could have as many wives as he liked, even 10 or more. When it was time to move on, they folded up the tents and packed them onto carts. Camels or **oxen** pulled the carts, carrying all of the family's possessions.

For food, the Mongols had a simple diet of meat and milk, provided by their animals. Marco reported: "They eat flesh of every description, horses, camels, and even dogs, provided they are fat."

### Mongol "porridge"

*Mongol riders made meals on the move. First, they skimmed the cream from boiling milk and allowed the milk to dry as a solid called milk curd. A lump of curd was added to water in a leather flask. Then, while riding through the day, the jolting mixed up the curd and water into a thick "porridge" for the evening meal.*

In the summer, Mongolian nomads still graze their goats, horses, and other animals on the grasslands and sleep in tents called *yurts*.

## Arrival in Hormuz

During 1272 the Polos traveled through the dangerous part of southern Iran between Kerman and Hormuz. This was the home of the terrifying Karaunas, where the Polos were attacked but escaped. Continuing south, they reached the port of Hormuz, in the Persian Gulf (see map on page 24).

The Polos looked in horror at the Arab boats called dhows. A dhow has one or two masts, slanting triangular sails, and a **rudder** for steering. The local wood was so hard that nails would split it. Instead, the dhow's planks were sewn together with a long-lasting cord made from coconut fiber. Oily fish fat was smeared over the planks as protection against sea water.

## An unsafe ship?

Marco could not believe that such a ship without nails was safe. Also, he was worried that the dhow had no iron anchor, so it might drift and be lost or wrecked. Marco wrote: "Great traders the citizens of Hormuz may be, but boatbuilders they are not!"

This Arab dhow dates from about 1880. Dhows are still used today for fishing, trading, and tourist trips around the Gulf, Red Sea, and East Africa.

In fact, the dhow is a well-designed ship that is still used today in the Middle East. But the Polos refused to sail in one. Instead, they decided to change their plans and head back north. They would join the overland trading route between China and Europe known as the Silk Road.

## The overland plan

Leaving Hormuz, the Polos retraced their steps to Kerman. This time, they arranged for guards to go ahead and watch for bandits. However, their new plan was very daring. They would have to climb high mountains, cross war zones, and encounter deadly diseases. Unlike today, in the 1200s there were no maps, lightweight tents, or sleeping bags, and there were only limited supplies.

Marco Polo described how Persians and other people made beautiful **silk** cloth, embroidered garments, and carpets—skills that are still widespread today.

### Iran (Persia)

*Iran used to be known as Persia. The Zagros Mountains cover much of its western half, and there are dry, flat deserts in the center. Since ancient times, local people have grazed sheep and goats. These animals' wool is made into beautifully decorated clothes, blankets, rugs, and carpets. Persian carpets were traded in Marco Polo's time and are still popular today.*

## Struck down by sickness

After Kerman, the Polos went through northern Persia, where Marco thought the women were "the most beautiful in the world." In 1273, during the second year of the trip, they reached Afghanistan. In sight of the awesome Pamir Mountains, Marco became sick with a disease called malaria. Exhausted and suffering from a high fever, one minute he was sweating, the next he was shaking with cold.

Niccolo and Matteo were desperate to continue the journey, but Marco could not move from his bed. It took him about a year to recover. Finally, Marco was able to walk once more, and the Polos began their journey into the mountains. The clean, cold air made Marco feel much better.

### Deadly diseases

*Malaria was only one of the deadly diseases common in Central Asia. Rat fleas spread plague, which caused high fever and lumps in the armpits. Leprosy damaged the skin and destroyed nerves, arms, legs, and eyes. Typhoid brought severe fever and pain, while smallpox caused high fever and marks on the skin. In those days, there was no cure for these diseases. Most people who caught them died.*

The Pamir Mountains form a huge barrier to travel in Central Asia. It is quite incredible that the Polos survived the climb.

## The roof of the world

In the mountains between Afghanistan and Tibet, the Polos made the tough climb to the Pamir **Plateau**. This high, flat area is called the "Roof of the World." Reaching the plateau is an enormous challenge even for today's climbers, who have modern equipment and oxygen supplies. The hazards include blizzards (severe snowstorms), avalanches (sudden falls of snow and ice), and rockfalls. Frostbite is a constant danger, as the cold freezes fingers and toes.

### Mountain air

*Marco noted that it took a long time to cook food in boiling water high in the mountains. He thought it was because of the cold. In fact, it is because of the lack of air at great heights. The reduced air pressure means water does not boil at the usual 212°F (100°C), but rather several degrees lower. Since the boiling water is less hot, cooking takes longer.*

# Toward the Silk Road

Near the eastern end of the Pamir Mountains, the Polos at last approached the Silk Road trading route. All kinds of wonderful goods were carried eastward, including gold, medicines, perfumes, **ivory**, and glassware. There were animals such as horses, camels, and sheep, and unusual creatures such as elephants and peacocks. **Slaves** were also there.

In exchange, the Chinese and Mongol people offered **silks**, spices, beautifully painted pottery, animal furs, **jade**, and bronze objects, which went westward. In addition to trading goods, travelers exchanged tales of faraway places.

In Mongol times, elephants were brought to China and used for ceremonies. The traditions continue today in India and nearby countries.

## Profits at every stage

Along the route, each **merchant** carried the goods a certain distance, then sold them for a small profit. The next merchant did the same, and so on. With no cars, trains, or planes, travel was tough and dangerous and took months. No wonder Eastern silks, spices, and precious gems were so expensive in Europe.

This 500-year-old scene shows Chinese merchants transporting pottery on the Silk Road. The picture is painted on silk cloth.

## The Silk Road at last

In 1274, more than three years after setting out from Venice, the Polos arrived in Kashgar (now Kashi, in the far west of modern China). At last, with remarkable strength and bravery, they had reached the Silk Road. Most travelers from the West sold their goods in Kashgar and then returned. But the Polos wanted to continue all the way to China.

## Into the desert

The next challenges for the Polos were the Takla Makan and Gobi Deserts. These bare lands had little water, few plants or animals to eat, and no shelter for travelers. It was wise to pick a route around the edge of the desert, passing through **oasis** towns where they could buy important supplies.

### Camels

*Asian travelers used camels to cross deserts. Camels are well suited to dry regions. They have tough mouths for eating thorny desert plants, and most of the water they need comes from their food. In summer they can go for 5 days without water, and in winter, 50 days! Their wide feet do not sink in soft sand, and they can close their nostrils to keep out windblown dust.*

## Days on the road

After leaving Kashgar, the Polos endured weeks in the desert. Each daybreak, they loaded up camels with goods and supplies. (The Polos also sometimes used donkeys, **mules**, and horses.) They planned the day's route, using a magnetic **compass** and the Sun's position for directions. If they were lucky, they found part of the route marked by stones. Sometimes they met other travelers and asked the way. When possible, they hunted animals, fished, and gathered plants. In towns they bought supplies from local markets.

Marco Polo wrote that Kashgar was an important city for trade, with lovely gardens, fruit trees, and vineyards for grapes to make wine. Today, the area is drier and more barren.

After each day's hard traveling, the Polos hoped to find a **caravanserai** (simple hotel or inn) where they could enjoy a comfortable night's sleep. These basic hotels, built along the trade routes of Asia, were welcome resting places. Visitors and their camels entered through a large gate into a wide courtyard. Around the sides were rooms where merchants could sleep. Travelers stocked up on food and water and could even trade there. But if there was no caravanserai, the Polos put up their heavy leather tents and camped overnight.

## Tackling the Takla Makan

In the winter of 1274, the Polos rested in the city of Lop and built up their strength for the bleak Takla Makan Desert. They probably traveled through the oasis to the south and east of the desert, where they could find water and more supplies.

## Lost and found

One day, Marco moved a short distance away from Niccolo and Matteo to look at a rock. The wind quickly blew away his tracks in the sand, and in an instant, he was lost. He knew that alone and without supplies, he would soon die. Frightened but calm, he waited patiently for rescue. Later that day his uncle found him, saving his life.

### Land of Death

*The Takla Makan Desert was a natural barrier to travel in Central Asia. It was so dangerous that local people called it the "Land of Death." They did not dare to enter the middle of the desert.*

## Thirty days in the desert

In early spring 1275, the Polos crossed the Gobi Desert. One of the world's largest deserts, the Gobi is mostly bare rock. The climate ranges from a freezing -40°F (-40°C) to a baking 113°F (45°C). The temperature can vary by as much as 58°F (32°C) in just 24 hours. It is like going through all the seasons of the year in just one day.

The Polos would need to survive for a month in the Gobi, with only the supplies that they could carry. They endured **sandstorms** blasting across the desert, extreme temperatures, hunger, and thirst.

## Noisy rocks and singing sands

The Polos were terrified by the stories of evil spirits that haunted the dry land and drew people away to their death in the sands. Local people claimed the Gobi Desert was haunted because they heard weird cracking noises and strange "singing." The cracking noises probably came from rocks, which expanded in the baking daytime heat and then shrank in the cold night. The "singing" was grains of sand blowing and tumbling with the shifting dunes.

Sandstorms happen when a strong wind picks up sand and dust from the ground and blows it around. It flies into people's faces, making it hard to see. It also covers tracks, paths, vehicles, and even buildings.

After 30 days in the desert, the Polos arrived in Dunhuang (then in Tibet, now part of China). Worn out, they rested for a while and traded with Tibetan people. The Polos were interested in the **Buddhist** faith of these local people. It was also a very welcome break after the great hardships of the Gobi Desert.

The city of Dunhuang, Tibet, was a main trading town for merchants traveling to China along the Silk Road.

### Flying Buddhists
*Many people in Tibet follow the teachings of the Buddha, who lived in ancient India. Marco claimed that he saw Tibetan Buddhist monks "fly." They were practicing levitation—being raised into the air without any aids. In fact, they had developed an athletic ability to leap up and remain in the air for a short time, almost as if flying.*

# The Land of the Great Khan

In spring 1275, four years after leaving Venice, the Polos traveled through Hami, part of Mongolia, and Manchuria (north of present-day Beijing). In a town near Hami, Marco Polo saw the people weaving an amazing material from a gray rock to form a white cloth that did not catch fire. It seemed magical. The material was **asbestos**. It was not used in the West until 600 years later.

## Asbestos

*Asbestos fiber comes from certain rocks. It can resist fire and was used in Western buildings from about 1800. In the late 1970s, scientists realized that breathing in asbestos fibers can cause lung cancer. It is now banned in many countries.*

The Polos spent almost four years traveling from their home in Venice to the marvelous palaces of Kublai Khan in China.

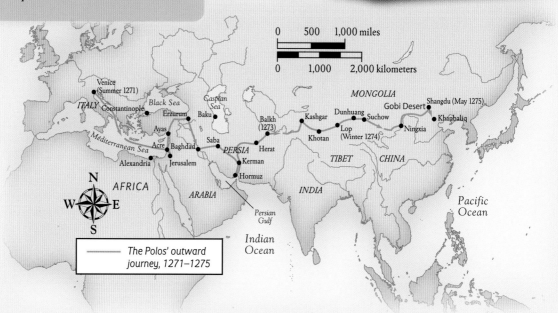

The Polos' outward journey, 1271–1275

## Kublai's welcome

The travelers knew they were close to Kublai **Khan**'s palace. One morning, they spotted a group of Mongol warriors in the distance following them. The Polos grew worried. After an exhausting four-year journey, would they now be killed on arrival?

As the Mongols grew closer, the Polos realized the Mongol warriors had no weapons. Soon, the strangers were being welcomed to the land of Kublai Khan. The great ruler had heard they were coming and had sent his men to help them find the palace.

## On foot to the palace

In May 1275, after another 40 days of walking, the Polos reached the Mongol court at Shangdu. Kublai Khan was delighted to see Niccolo and Matteo again. He accepted their gifts and prepared a feast. Marco was impressed by the fabulous palace, with its decorations of carved dragons, birds, beasts, and battle scenes and its beautiful lake and gardens.

The Polos greeted Kublai Khan and offered gifts to this all-powerful ruler.

### Musk

*As Marco traveled to Kublai Khan's palace, he smelled a strange perfume wafting through the air. It came from the musk ox, an animal that is similar to an antelope but the size of a goat. Some of its body parts were dried to make the perfume. Marco brought the dried head and feet of a musk ox back to Venice as souvenirs of his travels.*

## Marco and the Mongols

After their long journey, the Polos rested in China. They moved with Kublai Khan to his winter palace in Khanbaliq (now Beijing). Matteo and Niccolo probably continued their trade as **merchants**. But Marco quickly adopted Mongol customs and learned four new languages.

## Amazing discoveries

To the Polos, Kublai Khan was not a merciless killer, as he was described in Europe. He ruled a well-ordered society. Marco discovered useful inventions not known at home. For example, instead of exchanging gold or silver, the Mongols and Chinese used paper money, which was much easier to carry around. At any time, the owner could take the paper bills to a bank and exchange them for gold or silver.

Of course it was illegal for people to print their own money. In 1183 a printer who made 2,600 fake bills was put to death.

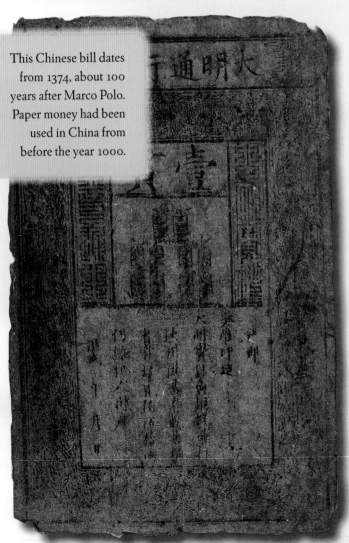

This Chinese bill dates from 1374, about 100 years after Marco Polo. Paper money had been used in China from before the year 1000.

## Letters and fires

There was also a postal service. Using teams of horses, important letters could be taken more than 250 miles (400 kilometers) in one day.

Marco described "a sort of black stone which burns—and gives out much more heat than wood." This was coal. It was known in Europe, but was not used much as fuel. In China it was mined and burned on a large scale in homes and small factories.

Kublai Khan took a great liking to Marco. The ruler liked to hear the tales about Marco's travels and adventures. Soon, Kublai decided to create a special mission for his new young friend. Marco was to travel around the **Mongol Empire** as the Khan's personal "spy." He would be the eyes and ears of the emperor in the Khan's vast lands and report back all of his findings.

### Kublai Khan (1215–1294)
*Kublai was the grandson of Genghis Khan. He conquered China and made it part of the enormous Mongol Empire. Although he was a powerful emperor, Kublai Khan remained a **nomad** at heart. He loved horses and liked to hunt bears and deer with trained leopards, **lynxes**, and even tigers.*

Kublai Khan traveled in great style. Here, he is in a luxury tent carried by elephants.

## An advanced society

Marco's spying missions for Kublai Khan began around 1276, when he was about 22 years old. Traveling through China, he saw amazing sights.

In eastern China the streets of Hangzhou (Hangchow) were paved with stone or brick. In Europe most streets were still dirt tracks. A **dam** had been built to change the river flow and prevent floods. The city even had a fire department. If a fire broke out, a guard sounded a gong and other guards rushed from all around to put out the flames.

Also in Hangzhou, beautiful cups, plates, and bowls were made from **porcelain**. Nobody yet knew how to make this fine pottery in Europe. A kind of stone was ground to powder, mixed with clay, and heated to a scorching 2,650°F (1,450°C) to make the object hard and strong.

### Dams

*A dam is a barrier across a river that holds back the water. There were many dams in ancient China made of huge banks of earth and stones. They were built to control flooding and to store water for drinking and watering crops. In modern times, the energy of the water is used to produce electricity.*

This porcelain plate, beautifully decorated with a fish and a flower, was made in China just before the time of Marco Polo.

## Crocodiles

Marco also traveled to Yunnan province in the far southwest of China. There he saw giant "serpents ... with claws like a tiger ... their jaws are wide enough to swallow a man, and their teeth are large and sharp." These were actually crocodiles, which were killed and had their body parts used as medicines.

In northern China, Marco saw groves of mulberry trees, which were food for silkworms. The Chinese produced their fine **silks** from these insects. The silkworm is the caterpillar of the silk moth. When it becomes a chrysalis, it spins silk for its cocoon. In Marco's time, Europeans did not know the secret of silk-making. Here is a basic method:

Silk is still made by pulling strands from a vat (tub) of silkworm cocoons.

### Silk secrets

1. *Boil the cocoons. Each cocoon has one thin fiber 3,000 feet (1,000 meters) or more in length.*
2. *Wind together the thin fibers from several cocoons onto a stick to form a thicker silken thread.*
3. *Weave the threads into smooth, soft, fine silk cloth. About 300 cocoons are needed to make one scarf.*

# In the Service of the Khan

After a few more years, Kublai **Khan** sent Marco Polo to explore beyond
the borders of the **Mongol Empire** and report back on everything he saw.
In 1285 Marco left from the large port of Zaitan (now Xiamen) on the east
coast of China. He traveled on a **junk**—a huge ship that could carry up to
300 people. The junk made the long, dangerous voyage south through the
South China Sea.

## Spice heaven

Arriving in Java, Indonesia, Marco could not believe his eyes. He saw trade in
pepper, nutmeg, cloves, and other immensely valuable spices. To a European
**merchant** who knew the price of such goods at home, it was a marvelous sight.

Marco moved on to Sumatra, another Indonesian island. He saw "a type of
monster beast" with a single horn in the middle of its forehead. He realized that
it was not a unicorn, an animal found only in stories. It was really a rhinoceros!

He also described small "men with tails . . . like those of a dog, but without
hair." These may have been the apes we call orangutans, a name that means
"person of the forest" in the local language. However, real orangutans have
no tails.

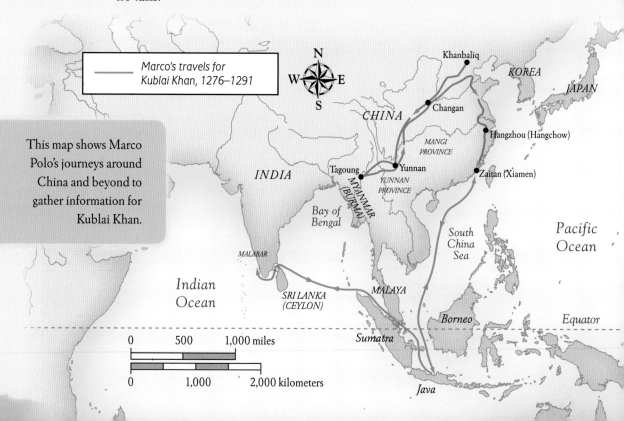

This map shows Marco Polo's journeys around China and beyond to gather information for Kublai Khan.

## Chinese junks

*These Chinese sailing vessels have been used for centuries. A junk has a flat-bottomed hull, four or five masts, and square sails made from panels of linen fabric flattened by bamboo strips. The sails can be spread or closed by pulling them like a modern window blind. During Marco Polo's time, Chinese sailors went to Indonesia and India in large seagoing junks.*

Junks of Marco Polo's time were used for trading along rivers and across seas. Some of the modern versions are pleasure and tourist boats.

## The disappearing North Star

In Sumatra, Marco noted that he could no longer see the **North Star** in the night sky. The position of the North Star is important to travelers and sailors because it shows the direction of true north. But it can only be seen in the Northern Hemisphere, which is the northern half of the world, above the Equator. Marco was now in the Southern Hemisphere, which is the southern half of the globe that is below the Equator.

## The ruby of Sri Lanka

From Sumatra, Marco sailed westward to Sri Lanka (formerly Ceylon). He saw breathtaking precious stones, including the most beautiful red rubies in the world. The king owned a grand ruby that was "as thick as a man's arm and a handspan in length." Kublai Khan had once desperately wanted this jewel. But the king refused to sell it for all the treasures that Kublai could offer.

Marco crossed from Sri Lanka to India. While he was there, he visited Malabar and Gujarat. He described rich farmland, where the people grew spices such as ginger and pepper, cotton for making cloth, and indigo for producing blue dye. They made fine cotton cloth and prepared animal skins for sale abroad.

## Rice and pirates

India, Sri Lanka, and countries of East and Southeast Asia depended on rice as their main food. Rice grows underwater in wet fields called paddies. In parts of Sri Lanka, there was not enough rain for the rice to grow. Farmers had to **irrigate** the land by flooding the fields from nearby rivers and lakes.

Marco also wrote about the cunning pirates around the coast of Gujarat, western India. They knew that merchants who were about to be captured often swallowed their jewels. When the pirates seized a merchant's boat, they forced him to drink sea water, which made his bowels open and release the jewels.

### The giant rukh

*From travelers' stories, Marco described the island of Madagascar, near Africa. It was supposed to be home to the rukh (roc), a gigantic bird with a **wingspan** of 50 feet (15 meters) that could seize an elephant with its talons (claws). Such tales were very unlikely. But scientists have discovered bones and eggs that show how an enormous flightless bird that was 10 feet (3 meters) high, called the elephant bird, once lived there.*

## Oysters and pearls

Along the coasts of Sri Lanka and India, skilled divers hunted for **oysters** containing **pearls**. They held their breath and went under water for about a minute at a time, putting the oysters in a bag or net tied to their body. The divers were so skilled that they could work all day.

This illustration from a 15th-century version of Marco Polo's book shows pearl fishing in Malabar, India.

# The Journey Home

After living for about 17 years in China, the Polos were homesick. They had grown rich from trading and wanted to return to Italy and enjoy their wealth.

They were in danger, too. Kublai **Khan** was nearly 80 years old, and likely to die soon. Many people at his court were jealous that the Polos were his special friends. Once Kublai was dead, the Europeans faced almost certain murder at the hands of these enemies.

## A princess to Persia

Then, an opportunity arose. Around 1292 Kublai Khan wanted to send 17-year-old Mongol Princess Kokachin to marry the Mongol Khan of Persia, Arghun Khan. The Polos offered to travel with the princess, and Kublai agreed. Since there were several wars raging between China and Persia, it was impossible to travel overland. They would go by ship from Zaitan.

To accompany Princess Kokachin, about 2,000 people sailed on 14 **junks** loaded with provisions (supplies) that could last two years. They used instruments such as the magnetic **compass** to find their way across the ocean.

Kublai Khan gave the departing Polos a golden tablet, like a Mongol "passport." It gave them the emperor's protection during their travels.

The expedition stopped off in Vietnam and the Malay Peninsula. Near Sumatra the ships battled against fierce storms and were forced to stop for five months. Setting sail once more, they traveled to Sri Lanka, then along the west coast of India and across the Indian Ocean to Hormuz, Persia—which the Polos had visited 20 years earlier.

During the 21-month journey from Zaitan to Hormuz, some passengers and sailors suffered deadly diseases such as **cholera** and **scurvy**. Others drowned or were murdered by pirates or hostile local people. Fewer than 1,400 people reached Hormuz.

The Polos' return journey from China to Venice was mainly by sea, unlike their outward trip.

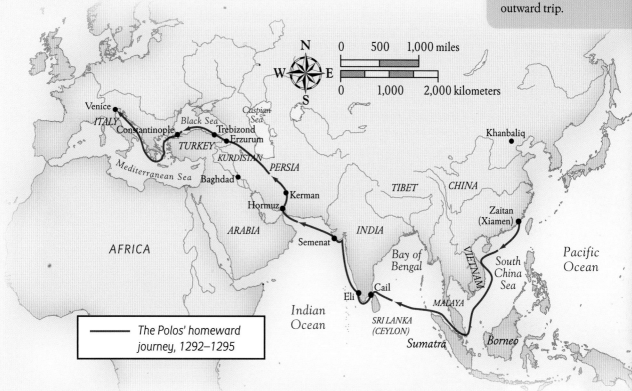

The Polos' homeward journey, 1292–1295

## Magnetic compass

*The magnetic compass was invented in China in around 1040. Earth is like a giant magnet, with north and south magnetic poles near the North and South Poles. The magnetic force of Earth makes the needle in the compass swing to a north–south position. Sailors, travelers, and explorers relied on the compass to find their route.*

## Delivering the princess

When the Polos and Princess Kokachin arrived in Hormuz in 1294, there was bad news. Arghun Khan had died. After frantic discussions, it was decided the princess could marry his son, Ghazan, instead. The princess cried when the Polos left, because they had become close friends on their long voyage. Then, there was a further shock. News from China said that Kublai Khan had died.

Saddened, the Polos continued their way overland from Hormuz back to Italy. In Trebizond, Turkey, robbers attacked them and gleefully seized valuable goods. Yet the **merchants**, expecting trouble, had cleverly hidden many jewels in their clothing.

### Foot-binding

*Marco Polo described many customs in China. But he did not mention that some Chinese girls had their feet bound tightly to keep them tiny. It was incredibly painful, but small feet were seen as a sign of beauty. Some people believed that because Marco did not mention some of these things, he had never really visited China.*

Marco Polo arrives in Hormuz in 1294, on his return to Italy. It is unlikely he really brought camels and elephants home!

## The homecoming

After three years of traveling, in 1295 the Polos finally reached Venice. One stormy night they banged on the door of their relatives, hoping for a warm welcome. Looking at the threesome, with their long beards, shabby clothes, and huge sacks of luggage, even the family members did not recognize Matteo, Niccolo, and Marco.

Hoping to convince the family that they really were the long-lost Polos, the three organized a grand dinner. They dressed in fine red satin cloaks from China. After eating a delicious meal, Marco brought the ragged, dirty clothes they had worn for their return. He ripped open the seams to reveal the most beautiful diamonds, rubies, sapphires, and other jewels that the Venetians had ever seen. This proved that they really were the Polos—and also that they were very rich.

## Journey times

It had taken the Polos three years to return home. Today, it is possible to fly the same journey, direct from Beijing in China to Venice in Italy, in fewer than 13 hours.

When the weary Polos reached Venice and knocked at their family's front door, at first their relatives did not let them in.

# Marco's Book

In 1298, three years after his return, Marco Polo commanded a warship during a conflict between Venice and another Italian city, Genoa. They were fighting over Mediterranean trade routes. Marco was captured and thrown into prison in Genoa.

Marco Polo's warship joined the battle against Venice's rival city of Genoa in 1298. It was common for a wealthy man to take command of a ship.

With time on his hands, Marco wrote down his adventures, with the help of a popular local writer named Rustichello. His book, *The Travels of Marco Polo*, was a mixture of what he had seen with his own eyes, other travelers' stories, and fantastic tales that he had heard.

When Venice and Genoa made peace in 1299, Marco was freed. He returned to Venice, where he married and had three daughters. His book was copied by hand for the few educated people who could read. They read it aloud to their families and friends. The book was a great success, and more copies spread around Italy like wildfire.

### Printing in China

*Marco's book had to be copied by hand because printing had not been invented in Europe. In fact, printing did exist in China, but Marco did not know about it. The text was written in ink and pressed onto a block of wood. Then, the wood was carved away from the un-inked part. The block was inked and pressed onto paper to form a print.*

## Il Milione

Marco's book became known as *Il Milione*, Italian for "a million." A similar word, *Emilione*, was the Polo family nickname. But *Il Milione* was also used to mock Marco's book, since some people claimed it told "a million lies."

## Tall tales?

Many people did not believe Marco's tales. Were there really rich cities in the East, giant birds, men with tails, or cloth that would not burn? Although Rustichello made the text more exciting, he did not invent stories himself. We now know that much of what Marco wrote was true.

As Marco lay dying in 1324, his friends wanted him to pass away with the truth on his lips. They asked if he had invented the tales in his book. Marco replied: "I have only told the half of what I saw."

This is the title page of the first printed edition of *The Travels of Marco Polo*, from 1477.

## Marco Polo—inspiring travelers

Marco Polo's book was the most important source of information about the world outside Europe in his time. He was not the first European to travel to China, but he was the first to write a detailed record of his journey.

A few European visitors traveled east, like the Polos. But after Kublai **Khan**'s death, the great **Mongol Empire** began to split. A Chinese family of rulers, the Ming **Dynasty**, took control of China in 1368. From around 1400 they banned European visitors and did not allow Chinese people to travel abroad. China stayed quite isolated from the rest of the world for hundreds of years.

## New information

In addition to writing a detailed record of the Mongol Empire at its peak, Marco wrote about the geography of the places he visited. His work was later used by European explorers. Some of his information was important in producing new maps. Yet much of the world remained unknown to Europeans. For more than a century after Marco's death, they still knew of only three continents—Europe, Asia, and Africa.

Marco's knowledge had another significant effect. European adventurers were excited by his stories of faraway lands rich in valuable spices. They decided to explore for themselves, in search of fame and fortune. Marco Polo inspired many others to travel the world.

### Noodles and pasta
*Marco Polo talked about the tasty noodles that were eaten in China. Some historians believe that his descriptions gave the Italians the idea to make pasta. However, others think that the Italians already knew how to make pasta.*

In 1492 Christopher Columbus reached the Caribbean, probably San Salvador. He had been encouraged by Marco's tales of adventure and discovery.

## Christopher Columbus

Italian-born sailor Christopher Columbus (1451 – 1506) led an
expedition of Spanish ships across the Atlantic Ocean in 1492.
Inspired by Marco Polo, he carried a copy of *The Travels* on this first
voyage. Columbus traveled west from Spain in the hope of reaching
India, China, and Japan. When he reached land, he thought he was in
India. Actually, he had reached the "New World" of the Americas.

# The Polos' Adventures in Asia

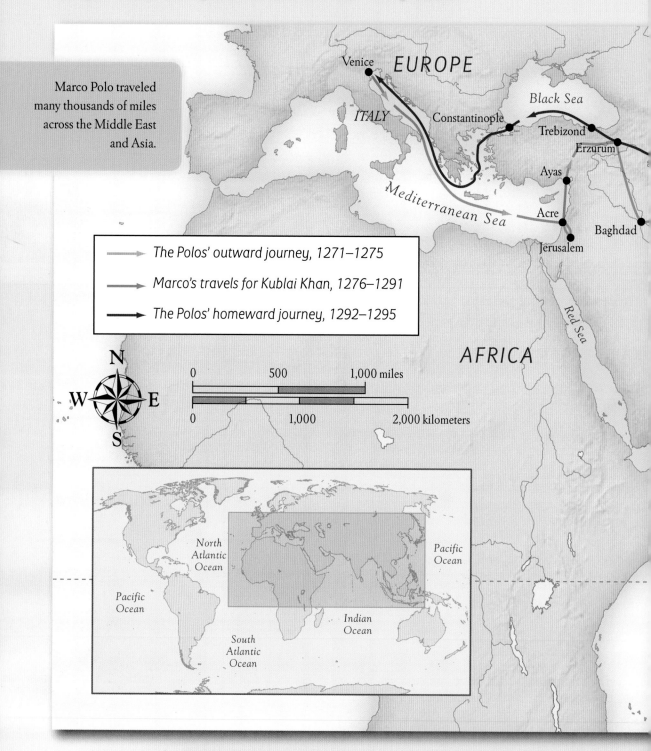

Marco Polo traveled many thousands of miles across the Middle East and Asia.

EUROPE

Venice

Black Sea

ITALY

Constantinople

Trebizond

Erzurum

Ayas

*Mediterranean Sea*

Acre

Baghdad

Jerusalem

Red Sea

⋯⋯⋯▶ The Polos' outward journey, 1271–1275

───▶ Marco's travels for Kublai Khan, 1276–1291

───▶ The Polos' homeward journey, 1292–1295

N W E S

0      500      1,000 miles

0      1,000      2,000 kilometers

AFRICA

North Atlantic Ocean

Pacific Ocean

Pacific Ocean

South Atlantic Ocean

Indian Ocean

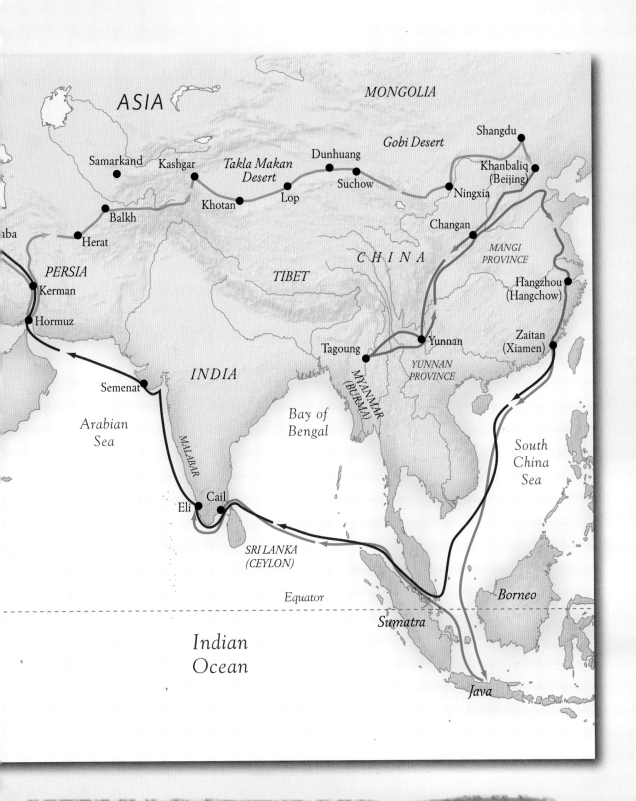

ASIA

MONGOLIA

*Gobi Desert*

Shangdu

Samarkand

Kashgar

*Takla Makan Desert*

Dunhuang

Khanbaliq (Beijing)

Khotan

Lop

Suchow

Ningxia

Balkh

aba

Herat

Changan

C H I N A

MANGI PROVINCE

*PERSIA*

Kerman

*TIBET*

Hangzhou (Hangchow)

Hormuz

INDIA

Tagoung

Yunnan

Zaitan (Xiamen)

Semenat

*YUNNAN PROVINCE*

*MYANMAR (BURMA)*

Arabian Sea

*MALABAR*

Bay of Bengal

South China Sea

Eli

Cail

*SRI LANKA (CEYLON)*

*Borneo*

Equator

*Sumatra*

Indian Ocean

*Java*

# Timeline

| | |
|---|---|
| **1253** | Niccolo and Matteo Polo leave Venice for Constantinople. |
| **1254** | Marco Polo is born, but his mother dies soon after . |
| **1259–1261** | Matteo and Niccolo set off from Constantinople to the Mongol lands and stay with Berke **Khan**, ruler of the western region. |
| **1265** | Matteo and Niccolo meet Kublai Khan, ruler of the **Mongol Empire**. |
| **1266** | Niccolo and Matteo leave to return to Venice. |
| **1269** | The Polos reach Venice in about April or May. |
| **Summer 1271** | Niccolo, Matteo, and Niccolo's son Marco leave Venice. The Polos arrive in the port of Acre (in modern-day Israel) and travel to Jerusalem. |
| **September 1271** | A new pope is elected, Gregory X. He calls on the Polos to return to Acre, where he blesses them and sends two **priests** with them on their mission. |
| **November 1271** | The Polos leave Acre to begin their overland journey to Hormuz. The priests abandon the mission. The Polos move through war-torn Armenia. |
| **1272** | Early in the year, the Polos probably pass through Erzurum in eastern Turkey and Tabriz in northern Iran, then Mosul and Baghdad in Iraq, and onward through Saba in Iran to Kerman. While traveling through the desert toward Hormuz, their **caravan** is attacked by robbers. The Polos reach Hormuz in the Persian Gulf, but decide not to travel by boat. They head north again toward the Silk Road. |
| **1273** | The travelers reach Afghanistan, where Marco becomes sick. They are forced to stop for about a year. |
| **Summer 1274** | The Polos travel over the Pamir Mountains from Afghanistan to Tibet. They reach Kashgar (now Kashi, China) and are now on the Silk Road. |
| **Winter 1274** | The Polos rest in Lop and then cross the Takla Makan Desert. |
| **Early 1275** | The travelers cross the Gobi Desert to Dunhuang, on the borders of ancient China. They rest and trade with the local people. |
| **Spring 1275** | The Polos travel through Hami, part of Mongolia, Manchuria, and Ningxia in China. |
| **May 1275** | The Polos reach the Mongol court at Shangdu and meet Kublai Khan. |

| | |
|---|---|
| **Winter 1275** | The Polos move to Khanbaliq (now Beijing) with Kublai Khan. |
| **1275** | Marco becomes a close friend of Kublai Khan. |
| **1276** | Marco sets off on his travels in the service of Kublai Khan. Over the next few years, he visits many places, including Hangzhou in eastern China and Yunnan province in the southwest. |
| **1285** | Marco leaves from Zaitan in eastern China, setting off by ship to travel outside the Mongol Empire. The ship stops at Java and Sumatra in Indonesia. Marco sails to Ceylon (now Sri Lanka) and India, where he visits Malabar and Gujarat. |
| **1292** | The Mongol Khan of Persia, Arghun Khan, sends a message to Kublai Khan, asking him to send a Mongol princess to be his wife. The Polos leave China by ship to accompany Princess Kokachin. |
| **1293** | After stopping in Sumatra for five months, the ships travel to Sri Lanka, along the west coast of India, and across the Indian Ocean. |
| **1294** | After a troubled voyage, the survivors arrive in Hormuz. The princess marries Ghazan, the new ruler. Kublai Khan dies. The Polos continue their voyage back to Italy. In Trebizond, Turkey, they are robbed. |
| **1295** | The Polos reach Venice safely. |
| **1298** | Marco Polo takes command of a warship during a conflict between Venice and Genoa. He is captured and sent to prison in Genoa. |
| **1298–1299** | In prison, Marco writes the story of his travels, with the help of a writer named Rustichello. |
| **1299** | Marco is freed and returns to Venice. The book of his adventures, *The Travels of Marco Polo*, is published. |
| **c. 1300** | Marco marries Donata Badoer. |
| **1324** | Marco Polo dies at age 70. In his will, he sets free his long-serving Mongol **slave**, Peter. |
| **1368** | The Ming **Dynasty** defeats the Mongol Empire in China. |
| **1400s** | China becomes an isolated country for many centuries. |

# Glossary

**archer** person who shoots arrows with a bow

**asbestos** mineral obtained from rocks that can be made into threads and fabrics that do not catch fire, but which harm health

**Buddhist** person who follows the teachings of the Buddha, who lived in India in ancient times

**caravan** group of traders and other people who travel across the desert together for safety

**caravanserai** basic hotel where travelers could stop and rest, especially on main routes across the Middle East and Asia

**cholera** disease caught from dirty water that causes vomiting and diarrhea and can kill

**compass** instrument with a needle that always points north–south that is used by sailors, explorers, and travelers to find directions

**dam** barrier across a river that holds back the water or makes it flow in a different direction

**dynasty** family of rulers who each pass on power to one of their children

**harbor** area of water along a coast that is protected from strong winds and big waves, where ships can take shelter

**holy oil** special oil used in religious ceremonies

**irrigate** bring water to an area of land through pipes or channels so that crops will grow

**ivory** hard white substance, like bone, that comes from the tusks of elephants and some other animals

**jade** hard green stone used to make ornaments and jewelry

**junk** traditional Chinese ship with a flat bottom and four or five masts and square sails

**khan** title given to a Mongol ruler

**lynx** wild cat with spots on its fur and a short tail

**merchant** person who trades, buying and selling goods in large amounts

**Mongol Empire** huge empire across Asia formed by the Mongols, nomads originally from Mongolia. It existed mainly in the 13th century.

**mule** animal that has a donkey and a horse as its parents and is used for carrying loads

**nomad** person who moves from place to place with his or her possessions, without a settled home

**North Star** bright star that can be seen directly above the North Pole

**oasis** area in the desert where there is water and plants grow

**oxen** (plural of "ox") bulls or cows that are mainly used for carrying or pulling loads

**oyster** large, flat shellfish; some kinds are very tasty and some produce shiny white jewels called pearls

**pearl** shiny, white, valuable jewel produced by some kinds of oysters and other shellfish

**plateau** wide area of flat land that is higher than the land around it

**porcelain** hard, white, shiny, pottery-type substance produced by baking clay and used to make delicate plates, cups, and ornaments

**priest** person who carries out religious duties—for example, in the Catholic Church, the main church in Europe during Marco Polo's time

**rudder** piece of wood at the back of a boat used for steering to control the boat's direction

**sandstorm** strong wind, especially in a desert, that whips up and carries clouds of sand and dust

**scurvy** disease caused by a lack of fresh fruits and vegetables in the diet

**silk** thin, strong fiber produced by silkworm caterpillars that is woven into smooth, soft cloth

**slave** person who is owned by another individual and is forced to work for that individual without pay

**steppe** large area covered with grass but no trees. In Asia, steppes stretch from Hungary in the west eastward to Manchuria in China.

**wingspan** distance between the tip of one wing and the tip of the other when the wings are fully stretched

# Further Information

## Books

Herbert, Janis. *Marco Polo for Kids: His Marvelous Journey to China*. Chicago: Chicago Review Press, 2001.
Lively writing with plenty of pictures and 21 activities about Marco Polo's journey.

McCarty, Nick. *Marco Polo: The Boy Who Traveled the Medieval World*. Washington, D.C.: National Geographic, 2006.
Tells the story of Marco Polo's journey and the discoveries he made in the context of the time period.

McNeese, Tim. *Marco Polo and the Realm of Kublai Khan*. Philadelphia: Chelsea House, 2006.
All about Marco Polo's years of travel in the service of Kublai Khan.

Zelenyj, Alexander. *Marco Polo: Overland to China*. New York: Crabtree, 2006.
An account of Marco Polo's travels that separates fact from myth using quotes from his book.

## Websites

www.metmuseum.org/explore/Marco/index.html
Follow Marco Polo's journey on this site by the Metropolitan Museum of Art, New York, viewing objects such as pottery, jewels, and weapons along the way.

http://afe.easia.columbia.edu/mongols/
This site, the "Mongols in World History," includes a section on life in China under Mongol rule.

## Places to Visit

American Museum of Natural History
Central Park West at 79th Street
New York, New York 10024-5192
Phone: (212) 769-5000
Website: www.amnh.org

At the American Museum of Natural History, you can find out about peoples and cultures from around the world, including the regions Marco Polo visited.

The Mariners' Museum
100 Museum Drive
Newport News, Virginia 23606
Phone: (757) 596-2222
Website: www.mariner.org

The Mariners' Museum's permanent exhibition "Age of Exploration" follows historical developments in shipbuilding, ocean navigation, and mapmaking. See displays of ship models, books, illustrations, maps, navigational instruments, and more.

The Metropolitan Museum of Art
1000 Fifth Avenue
New York, New York 10028
Phone: (212) 535-7710
Website: www.metmuseum.org

The Metropolitan Museum of Art has one of the world's most extensive collections of artifacts and art from around the world, including the places Marco Polo visited.

11/9/11-3

# Index

Acre 8, 9, 42, 44
Afghanistan 16, 44
Arghun Khan 34, 36, 45
Armenia 9, 44
asbestos 24

Baghdad 10, 44
Buddhists 10, 23

camels 4, 13, 18, 19, 20, 21
China 5, 6, 7, 9, 19, 23, 24,
    26, 28, 30, 34, 40, 41, 43,
    44, 45
Christianity 8, 9, 10
coal 26
Columbus, Christopher 41
compass 21, 34, 35
Constantinople (Istanbul) 6,
    42, 44
crocodiles 29

dams 28
dhows 14–15
diseases 15, 16, 35
Dunhuang 23, 43, 44

Genghis Khan 7, 27
Genoa 38, 45
Ghazan 36, 45
Gobi Desert 19, 22–23, 44
Gregory X, Pope 9, 44
Gujarat 32, 45

Hami 24, 44
Hangzhou (Hangchow) 28, 43,
    45
Hormuz 14, 15, 35, 36, 43,
    44, 45

India 32, 33, 35, 43, 45
Indonesia 30, 45
Iran see Persia
Iraq 10, 44
irrigation 32

Java 30, 43, 45
Jerusalem 8, 42, 44
junks 30, 31, 34

Karaunas 4, 5, 14
Kashgar (Kashi) 19, 20, 43, 44
Kerman 14, 15, 16, 43, 44
Khanbaliq (Beijing) 7, 26,
    43, 44
Kokachin, Princess 34, 36, 45
Kublai Khan 7, 8, 9, 10,
    24–25, 26, 27, 28–29, 30,
    34, 36, 40, 44, 45

Lop 21, 43, 44

Malabar 32, 33, 43, 45
malaria 16
Malay Peninsula 35
Manchuria 24, 44
merchants 6, 18, 19, 26, 30,
    32, 36
Ming Dynasty 40, 45
Mongol Empire 6, 7, 10, 27,
    30, 40, 44, 45
Mongolia 24, 44
Mongols 7, 11, 12–13, 18,
    24, 25
Mosul 10, 44
Mount Ararat 10
Muslims 10

Pamir Mountains 16, 17, 18, 44
pasta 40
pearl diving 32, 33
Persia (Iran) 4, 10, 14, 15, 16,
    34, 35, 43, 44, 45
Peter, slave 5, 45
pirates 8, 32, 35
Polo family 44,
    China 6–7, 8–9, 10, 24, 25,
    26–27, 43
    Gobi Desert 22–23
    Hormuz 14, 43, 44

Iranian Desert 4–5
    Pamir Mountains 16–17
    return home 34–37, 42–43
    Silk Road 18–19
    Takla Makan Desert 20–21
Polo, Marco 5, 8, 42–43, 44
    book 5, 38–41
    spies for Kublai Khan 27,
    28–29, 30, 32, 43
Polo, Matteo (Maffeo) 4, 6–7
Polo, Niccolo 4, 6–7

Rustichello 38, 45

Saba 10, 44
Shangdu 25, 44
silk production 29
Silk Road 15, 18, 19, 23, 44
slaves 5, 18
South China Sea 30, 43
Spice Route 6
spice trade 30
Sri Lanka (Ceylon) 32, 35,
    43, 45
Sumatra 30, 31, 32, 35,
    43, 45

Takla Makan Desert 19, 21,
    43, 44
The Travels of Marco Polo 38,
    41, 45
Tibet 23, 43, 44
Trebizond 36, 42, 45
Turkey 6, 10, 36, 44, 45

Venice 5, 6, 7, 8, 35, 37, 38,
    42, 44, 45

yurts 13

Zaitan (Xiamen) 30, 34, 35,
    43, 45